LA JOLLA COUNTRY DAY SCHOOL

3 3676 00023 1769

D0432170

DATE DUE

FEB 17 1997	OCT 05 2000
APR 16 1997	
SEP 10 1998	JAN 17 2001
NOV 20 1997	JUN - 9 2001
APR 19 1999	SEP 27 2001
MAR 07 2016	OCT 26 2001
SEP 20 2000	DEC 13 2001
SEP 01 2004	MAY 06 2002
NOV 13 2000	SEP 23 2002
	OCT 9 2003
NOV 01 2002	

THE LIBRARY STORE   #47-0120

LA JOLLA COUNTRY DAY SCHOOL
LIBRARY
9490 Genesee Ave.
La Jolla, CA 92037

BARRY
BONDS

LA JOLLA COUNTRY DAY SCHOOL
LIBRARY
9490 Genesee Ave.
La Jolla. CA 92037

(Photo on front cover.)

In 1990, Barry Bonds became the first Pirate to have more than 30 home runs and 30 stolen bases in a season.

(Photo on previous pages.)

Bonds steals home against the New York Mets.

Text copyright © 1996 by The Child's World, Inc.
All rights reserved. No part of this book may be reproduced
or utilized in any form or by any means without written
permission from the Publisher.
Printed in the United States of America.

Photography supplied by Wide World Photos Inc.

Library of Congress Cataloging-in-Publication Data
Rambeck, Richard.
Barry Bonds / Richard Rambeck.
p. cm.
Summary: Relates the baseball career of this San
Francisco Giant who had been with the Pittsburgh Pirates
and who was three times named the National League's
Most Valuable Player.
ISBN 1-56766-201-3 (lib. bdg.)
1. Bonds, Barry. 1964- —Juvenile literature.
2. Baseball players—United States—Biography—
Juvenile literature. [1. Bonds, Barry, 1964- .
2. Baseball players. 3. Afro-Americans—Biography.]
I. Title
GV865.B637R36 1995   95-6460
796.357'092—cd20   CIP
[B]   AC

BARRY
BONDS

BY RICHARD RAMBECK

**Bonds waves
to his father,
Giants' first
base coach
Bobby Bonds.**

During the 1992 baseball season, it looked as though the San Francisco Giants wouldn't be playing in San Francisco much longer. The team's owner was ready to sell the club to a group of businessmen who planned to move it to Florida. The Giants franchise, which had moved from New York to San Francisco in 1957, seemed to be on the verge of changing homes again. Just in time, though, a group of San Francisco businessmen agreed to buy the Giants.

To their fans' delight, the Giants would remain in San Francisco, but the new owners knew they had a lot to do to turn the club's fortunes around. In 1992, the Giants finished with a 72–90 record and wound up fifth in the six-team National League West Division. The new owners, led by Peter Magowan, soon had a surprise for the San Francisco fans. The team signed the best player in the game, left fielder Barry Bonds of the Pittsburgh Pirates.

Bonds leaps high for one while playing for the Pittsburgh Pirates.

Bonds had led the Pirates to three straight NL East Division championships. He was voted Most Valuable Player of the National League in 1990 and 1992. When the 1992 season ended, so did Bonds' contract with the Pirates. He was a free agent and could sign with

Bonds receives encouragement from his father.

any team. He chose the Giants. Why? Barry's father, Bobby Bonds, had been a star for San Francisco in the 1970s. In addition, Barry's godfather was former Giants star Willie Mays.

When he signed with the Giants, Barry Bonds said he felt like he was going home. The team was giving Bonds a lot of money to go home — his contract was for more than $40 million, the richest in baseball history. Bonds, however, would soon start earning his keep. Faced with the pressure of being so highly paid, he responded like a champion. He had the best year of his career in 1993, and that's saying a lot.

Led by Bonds, the Giants jumped to the top of the NL West standings and stayed there for most of the 1993 season. His teammates gave Bonds a lot of the credit for the team's improvement. "When Barry signed with us, I didn't know what to expect," said San Francisco second baseman Robbie Thompson. "Then I watched him play. I have never seen a player who dominated the way he did. It was like he was playing among Little Leaguers."

It was almost impossible to stop Barry Bonds in 1993. He led the National League in home runs with 46. He also had an NL-best 123 runs batted in. Both

Bonds once hit two three-run homers against the Los Angeles Dodgers.

San Francisco's Bonds is safe at third.

were career highs for Bonds. "He can pretty much do it all," said San Francisco pitcher Jeff Brantley. "He can hit for average, power, run the bases, and play strong defense. And he's not just trying to get a hit. He's trying to crush the ball. If you make a bad pitch, he'll hit a home run."

Near the end of the 1993 season, the Atlanta Braves moved ahead of the Giants and into first place. Bonds, however, wouldn't let San Francisco fade. As they entered the final weekend of the season, the Giants moved into a tie for first with Atlanta, but then they lost two of three games to the Los

Angeles Dodgers to finish one game behind the Braves. Bonds still was voted National League MVP for the third time in his career.

Bonds signs autographs before the 1993 All-Star Game.

Despite his MVP award, Bonds wasn't satisfied. For the fourth year in a row, his team had fallen just short of winning a championship. When he was with Pittsburgh, the Pirates had made it to the NL Championship Series in 1990, 1991 and 1992 — and lost all three times. "Ever since I started playing baseball, all the way from Little League, I've been to every championship I could possibly go to," Bonds said. "And I've always lost."

**Bonds listens
to his
godfather,
Hall of Famer
Willie Mays.**

Bonds might not have won any championships, but he's always been an outstanding player. After a highly successful college baseball career at Arizona State University, he was picked by the Pirates in the first round of the 1985 amateur draft. Pittsburgh sent Bonds to the minor leagues, but he didn't stay there very long. In 1986, Pirates General Manager Sid Thrift was watching Bonds take batting practice.

As Thrift watched, Bonds hit ten homers to right field. Thrift walked up to Bonds and said, "Any left-handed hitter can hit the ball over the right field fence. Why don't you hit some over the center field and left field fences." Bonds got back into the batter's box and started slamming homers to left and center. As he walked to the dugout, Bonds looked at Thrift, smiled, and said, "That's what you wanted, right?"

Left fielder Bonds tosses the bat after striking out in the All-Star Game.

Thrift knew Bonds was ready to play for the Pirates. Bonds spent most of the 1986 season with Pittsburgh. From 1986 to 1989, he was a solid player for the Pirates, but not a star. That would change, though, during the following season. In 1990, Bonds became the first major leaguer ever to hit more than .300 and have at least 30 home runs, 100 RBI, and 50 stolen bases in a

Bonds watches his second three-run homer of the game as it leaves the ballpark.

season. His performance earned Bonds his first National League MVP award.

Bonds had become one of the best players in the game, but his goal was to win, not to be famous. "I'm not comfortable being at the center of things," he said. "I don't need that. I appreciate the ability I've been given, but all I want to do is win." But Bonds doesn't want just to win. His teams have already been winners. What he really wants is to win a championship, which is about the only thing in baseball he hasn't achieved yet.